THE EDUCATION OF MAN

Aphorisms

PESTALOZZI AND THE ORPHANS IN STANS
Oil painting by A. Anker, 1870, in the possession of the Kunsthaus, Zurich

Johann HEINRICH PESTALOZZI

THE EDUCATION OF MAN

Aphorisms

With an Introduction by

WILLIAM H. KILPATRICK

GREENWOOD PRESS, PUBLISHERS
NEW YORK

PESTALOZZI AS EDUCATOR

Johann Heinrich Pestalozzi (1746–1827) was in his day the world's most widely acclaimed teacher of the young. Today it seems further fair to assert that Pestalozzi stands out as the one man who more than any other in educational history succeeded in shifting educational aims and procedures from a long prevailing faulty pattern to a distinctly different pattern which has since brought outstanding better results and still promises indefinite growth.

No creation comes from a vacuum. Pestalozzi was a child of the eighteenth century Enlightenment, that movement which in America produced Pestalozzi's close contemporary, Thomas Jefferson (1743–1825). As Jefferson, the advocate of political freedom and equality, wrote our Declaration of Independence and later guided free America along the line of its democratic respect for individuality, so Pestalozzi carried the same Enlightenment spirit of equality of opportunity and respect for human personality into the schoolroom, where beforetimes these had been conspicuously and sadly lacking.

Three things in the school practice of his time deeply stirred Pestalozzi: first, that the children of the poorest were in effect excluded from education; second, that in school a "superficial verbosity," as he called it, characterized pupil recitation, they hardly knew the meanings of the words they recited and accordingly failed both in spirit and in fact; third, that these children were flogged unmercifully for failing even though the failure was not their fault. It was these three school practices that Pestalozzi directly attacked.

Six principles eventually emerged for Pestalozzi as he sought to remake the school effort. (The wording here except in direct quotations is of our day.)

1. Personality is everywhere sacred. This constitutes the "inner dignity" of each individual, for the young as truly as for the adult.

2. As "a little seed . . . contains the design of the tree," so in each child is the promise of his potentiality. "The educator only takes care that no untoward influence shall disturb nature's march of developments."

3. Love of those we would educate is "the sole and everlasting foundation" in which to work. "Without love, neither the physical nor the intellectual powers will develop naturally." So kindness ruled in Pestalozzi's school; he abolished flogging—to the amazement of all outsiders.

4. To get rid of the "verbosity" of meaningless words Pestalozzi developed his fundamental doctrine of *"Anschauung,"* direct concrete observation, often inadequately called "sense perception" or "object lessons." In his school no word was to be used for any purpose until adequate *Anschauung* had preceded. The thing or

the distinction must somehow be seen or felt or otherwise observed in the concrete. Pestalozzi's followers developed from this the commonly recognized principles: from the known to the unknown, from the simple to the complex, from the concrete to the abstract—principles which the pre-Pestalozzian schools tragically disregarded.

5. To perfect the perception got by the *Anschauung*, the thing must be named, and appropriate *action* must follow. "A man learns by action . . . have done with [mere] words!" "Life shapes us and the life that shapes us is not a matter of words but action."

6. Apparently out of this demand for action came an emphasis on repetition—never blind repetition, repetition of action following the *Anschauung*. (This particular repetition as used by Pestalozzi seems to us now undesirably formal.)

Pestalozzi's school run on these principles attracted wide attention and at its height brought him great fame. Many famous people and inquiring minds came to see the school with their own eyes. Strange in that day was it to see a school succeed, succeed greatly, where there was no whipping and real friendliness held between master and child, with self-activity on the part of the pupils and great interest in all they did. It was literally true that those who came to scoff returned to praise. Many were the ambitious young men who came to study with Pestalozzi, two of whom later greatly influenced American education, Froebel (1782–1852) and Herbart (1776–1841).

Historically, the greatest single effect from Pestalozzi influence was on the *Volksschule* of Prussia. After the downfall at Jena (1806) Prussia made a determined effort to create a new life. Wilhelm von Humboldt, a great scholar and statesman, was put at the head of education. On the advice of Fichte that Pestalozzi's method was the only suitable one to use, a number of Prussian young men were sent thither with instructions to "give themselves completely up . . . to the life and pedagogical activity which are nowhere so busy as there." These young men did as they were told and returned to Prussia to remake the *Volksschule* and to institute seminaries for teacher training. The result was that the world at large came to look upon these Prussian schools as the best anywhere to be found. The French philosopher, Victor Cousin, made (1831) a careful study of these Prussian schools and seminaries and wrote a report which had great influence on the French educational reconstruction of 1833. This report was translated into English and spread widely through the United States. The husband of Harriet Beecher Stowe, Calvin Ellis Stowe (1837), and Horace Mann (1843) also made reports of their study of the Prussian schools. It seems safe to affirm that the great remaking of American education from 1830 to 1860 came directly or indirectly from Pestalozzi, much of it by way of Prussia. From this source came our first normal schools. From Pestalozzian influence the American schools took on geography, music, art, gymnastics; arithmetic teaching was remade to be understandable by children; the word method of teaching reading supplanted the cumbersome old alphabet method; whipping was increasingly abolished.

Various persons brought the Pestalozzian school methods to America. Joseph Neef (1770–1854), who had taught with Pestalozzi, was brought to America to teach these methods. He taught in the East and the Middle West from 1806 to the time of his death. The Western Literary Institute, of which Calvin Ellis Stowe was a member, worked from 1831 at extending the general Pestalozzian outlook. More widely known was "the Oswego movement," a systematic effort in the third quarter of the century to spread the better features of Pestalozzianism. Helping Dr. E. A. Sheldon in this was Herman Krusi, Jr., son of Pestalozzi's most famous assistant of the same name. It has been claimed that the "culminating point" of Pestalozzian influence in this country was reached when William T. Harris introduced its method into the St. Louis public schools during his superintendency of 1867–80. In the judgment of this author, however, a higher point was reached at Quincy, Massachusetts, 1876–80, under Colonel Francis W. Parker. This was pretty certainly the highest point before Herbartianism was introduced about

1890 and Dewey's influence began about 1895.

As a conclusion attention may be called to a certain respect in which Pestalozzi seems to have anticipated some of the most advanced thinking of our day, philosophical and educational. He counted that "our powers of understanding are best developed" in practical affairs "where every blunder and every omission shows up on the spot." Peirce, James, and Dewey have held that meanings and understanding relate precisely to "natural events," that "the meaning of an idea consists of the particular consequences to which it leads." Modern education says that "we learn what we live" and then use that learning in more pertinent living.

Pestalozzi, as just said, held that we best develop meanings and understanding in life situations. This brings out and shows up on the spot the adequacies and inadequacies of our thinking. He further said that "life itself is the true basis of teaching and education" and still further that "life shapes us and the life that shapes us is not a matter of [mere] words, but of action." And our most modern education holds that, since the child will learn what he lives, the school must be a place of living; and we would add here with Pestalozzi that that life lived must include action of a kind to test the pupil's thinking. In this way does Pestalozzi seem to anticipate the modern school that we now most acclaim.

WILLIAM HEARD KILPATRICK

October 2, 1950

TABLE OF CONTENTS

	Introduction, by William H. Kilpatrick	vii
I	Mankind and Humanity	1
II	The Individual	11
III	Home and Hearth	21
IV	The Education of Man	29
V	Man among Men	39
VI	Of Poverty, the Sacred	49
VII	Justice and Liberty	57
VIII	Truth and Wisdom	65
IX	Chips and Shavings	71
X	Nature, the World, and God	83

THE EDUCATION OF MAN

Aphorisms

I

Mankind and Humanity

1 · MANKIND AND HUMANITY

I TAKE NO PART in men's quarrels about their opinions. But when their deeds are marked by true devotion and plain-spoken faith, when the love of God and of their neighbors dwells in their hearts, bringing blessed happiness to their homes, I hold that these things should, of rights, be beyond dispute to all of us, should be enshrined in our own hearts.

He who seeks out, with faith and fervent sincerity, all that is sacred and exalted in human nature, will gain a God-like power over all that is divine within us, shedding warmth and light upon any man receptive to the sacred and divine, as God's own sun pours down upon the earth.

He who bears the interests of humanity in his breast, that man is blessed.

Not for me, but for my brethren, not for mine own self, but for the human race, thus speaks the untrammeled divine voice within us; only in hearkening to it, in obeying it, do we find such nobility as human nature holds.

Hold firm to your faith in the inner concert of the good, in its power to stiffen all other good on which it touches. Thereby will you foster in it the power to kindle further, loftier and undreamed of good which, in its results, will wield the same quiet but triumphant strength over the powers of evil, as a new tooth in the mouth expels the old one, roots and all, supplanting it as though it had never been there.

The salvation of the world is a civilized humanity.

There is in us a sacred and divine presence, which a man can cherish and foster on his own, thus rising to the inner dignity of his nature, the only means by which he can truly become a man.

What roots are to a growing tree, faith and charity —the powers of the heart—are to a man, in that he is a divine and immortal being that must be trained and educated.

Love is the sole and everlasting foundation on which our nature can be trained to humaneness.

Hard-heartedness is at the core of all human iniquity.

Sooner or later, but of a certainty in the end, Nature will take her toll for what men do against her.

The good instincts of mankind, in their pure state, are more than gifts of art or chance. Their fundamental qualities lie deeply buried in man's nature. All men feel the need to develop these powers and the paths along which Nature reveals them, must be kept clear and easy of access. To achieve wisdom and tranquillity, the processes of human education must be kept simple and of universal application.

At every level, a servant is like unto his master in his essential character, and the master owes his servant the opportunity to satisfy his nature's needs.

The stature of a serf is likewise that of humankind.

For those quarters of the globe that are morally, spiritually and politically on the decline, there can be no salvation save through education, through training for humanity, through human culture.

Empires may perish and nations wither but human nature endures, and the laws that govern it are everlasting.

Let us become human beings, that once again we may be citizens and nations.

The smile of happiness, the tear of sympathy, are both denied the world of beasts. They are the privilege of mankind alone. Theirs is a hushed speech, common to all and apprehended by all, since it is felt by all.

Men hold laughter sacred—unless they be fools or knaves.

To mark the days by which we grow, God lets loftiest exaltation alternate with heart-rending sorrow; but the point is not whether such days are happy or freighted with grief; their sole purpose is to make us grow.

How can the spirit of good enter in, it has been asked, unless evil first be driven out? We prefer to put it this way: how can the spirit of evil be expelled, save by the good?

If you fight evil rather than do good it shall avail you nothing on the good side; quite the contrary, you will be running your head against a wall, all on behalf of evil. If circumstances run counter to the nature of your final purpose, all the more reason why you must hold to doing good alone, passing over evil as though it were not there; all the more reason why you must not swerve from the goal, but strive toward it with sufficient husbanded strength, secure in the power of love and truth.

To accomplish good in this our world takes more, much more, than merely to suggest it, dreamlike, to the human soul, that it marvel thereon, and glory in the image; men must be brought to pick out the thread by which the good thus shown them will ultimately lay rein upon their inner life, their inclinations, and their aspirations; and, as it were, take over their eyes, their hands, their tongues, and all their outward powers.

Only the good that still dwells in us can help us attain the ever greater good we lack.

The man who could do good and does not do it, is the greater sinner.

Thousands upon thousands would fain be good, if they but knew how, if they but had the strength and the impulse, if but a helping hand were offered them.

Many who rave and rant do so only because their love has been scorned and their faith mocked.

˙ Hundreds of wretched men are lost for the want of someone who might rouse them to a sense of their inner worth.

We can do nothing through enlightenment, save to give free scope to the good that is already present in the land, and to put obstacles in the way of the evil that is equally real.

Man of himself is good, and desires to be good, but he wishes to be happy when doing it; if he happens to be evil, surely it is because the road by which he sought to do good was blocked.

The world is full of useful people, but void of those who will give the useful man a job.

A noble soul is duty-bound by love and good deeds, quite as much as by law and justice.

Is any heroism greater than that by which a man rises above a sorrow that would put another in his grave? Or silences the rancor that perturbs his days, praying for his bitter foe as he might for the child of his own heart?

It is well to be a little like a child—to believe, to trust, to love, to turn away from errors, faults and follies, to be better and simpler-minded than the knaves, and through their very malice to become wiser than they. In spite of all we see and hear, it is a boon to think the best of men, and though we daily find ourselves mistaken, to trust the human heart ever and again, to forgive the wise men and the fools who, both of them, are all too likely to lead us astray.

People will never hesitate to let you help them, if you but know how to go about it; for anyone will gladly climb a ladder if he but sees that he can scale it safely.

What good is all the talk about the evils of our time, unless we are shaken to our very roots? What good does us the outer light of truth, if we lack the inner light of sympathy?

When men tremble for their fellows, who will be bold enough to charge them with running counter to God's commandments? When common men speak with tongues of burning fire of those in the land who are poor, wretched and neglected, who is to charge them with subversion?

O ye fortunates! Sacred flares the flame of those who cry forever in the wilderness, who, suffering with the lowly and disfranchised, come to speak in accents of despair. Their speech is like a shadow of heavenly truth, like a faded token of man's divine nature.

Whoever forthrightly considers the primary concerns of humankind; who freely and valiantly entrusts the full weight of their validity to the scales of justice, in counterpoise to outmoded opinions—such a one will always find himself opposed. Jesus Christ himself, who as a God-man spoke not only divinely for the poor and weak, but suffered and died divinely, aroused the greatest opposition with his truth and love. He knew it well, for He said Himself: "Think not that I am come to send peace on earth: I am not come to send you peace, but a sword." But for all that He foresaw this strife, He never stifled the least of his loving, divine pursuits.

The most momentous events of history are always things accomplished that had been held to be impossible. It is vain to try to set a limit to the surge of genius; still more hopeless is it to set limits to the ultimate effects of good will.

Getting together is the means by which anything can be accomplished.

Harmony cannot be brought about by unity, but unity must be attained through harmony.

People of good will are at bottom never very far apart; they will always meet, once they have been able to declare themselves.

In the hand of God even the evil-doer is an instrument for doing good; even in the midst of doing wrong a higher power forces him to promote the good. He knows not that he does so; but in the end, the evil he desired will have vanished, and the good that God willed will be there.

True, a man may for a time exist with neither faith, nor love, nor reason, nor pursuit; but his capacity for faith, love, reason or work will never altogether die within him. When from above one makes the right appeal to the good that is in the human heart, surely the heart will open.

Our hearts must live, work and endure—that is what matters, not that they should glitter.

The heart lends color to all that men see, and hear, and know.

Whatever I may be, I am by virtue of my heart.

Our earth is heaven if we but seek peace, do right, and ask for little.

II

The Individual

Each one of us must set himself a goal he cannot reach, that he forever must needs struggle and strive.

My child, this world is wicked. Fear its favors, fear its charms, fear its gold. But most of all, fear your own weakness.

Fear not to know yourself. There is on earth no way to wisdom, no way to happiness, save through self-knowledge.

The greatest victory a man can win is victory over himself.

Who spurs himself goes farther than who spurs the fleetest steed.

Whoever you be, look to yourself for truth and love, for the power to resist your greedy self and its senses. Though these powers be found nowhere else, you will find them within; they dwell in you as part of God, as they dwell in all who want and seek them.

A man's own strength is the only true foundation of his fortunes; his heritage is but the cradle that rocks him to sleep, until all opportunity has passed.

What is there left to us in the end but the value we put upon ourselves? And what is a man's worth, unless it be his skill to do as much as possible, his ability to be content with little, and his resolve to let nothing go untried?

O noble will of man! To you I bow down. I am a man only because I can will.

Man's will, the essence of his capacity to absorb the good and bad in human nature, is free. Man is blessed with a conscience.

As a man respects himself, so he will respect his own nature in other men. Self-respect is the true means for uniting mankind.

He who fails to look down on himself holds none of his failings cheaply.

It has been my experience that here on God's green earth no one will help a man, indeed, can help him, unless he can help himself.

If we want things to go better, in the humblest cottage as in the world at large, we must ourselves do what we can to help. I think it sacrilege to hold that God should do it for us, without our help, and in our stead.

The whole of our morality consists of our knowledge, our practice, and our desire of the good.

A man should know not only what is true, he should also be able to do and to desire what is right.

Cultivation of the intellect will not ennoble a man, unless it is founded on cultivation of the heart.

The great lesson of true happiness in life is, that a man must do right for his own sake, not to please others.

The good man sees every incident of his life as a God-sent means to perfect himself.

God helps those who are really willing.

It does no good to strut and swagger when one is weak.

A man can do infinitely much if only he is willing.

Men grow great and strong in all innocence, without effort or show; no sooner do they strain for effect than they lose their spontaneity and grow weak.

I am made up of physical, social and moral forces. The first arises from my animal nature; the second from my association with my fellows; but the third solely from my innermost strivings for virtue.

To let work and business give way to the call of duty is perhaps the most tempting self-delusion on earth.

No matter how much your affairs may be confused and disordered, if you but have the courage to speak the truth without reserve, you can always attack the evil, and, in one way or another, peace and quiet will return to you in the end.

Resolution in adversity is always half the battle for salvation.

It is only human to gloss over a minor slip by hook or crook. But in so doing, one must take care, lest the minor slip lead all the way to murder and arson.

Only a good conscience always gives man the courage to handle his affairs straightforwardly, openly and without evasion.

Do not forget grave and weighty duties over some minor commitment. Our first and most important duty is to watch ourselves, and guard our own hearts.

If only you are serious about playing fair, nothing else will count for much. One man's voice may be faint, another's strong—no matter. What counts is the use to which he puts his voice.

Good folk will complain but little. The man who whimpers is not worth his salt. A good heart always knows its worth, and if a man have any value in him, experience and hardship will enhance it. What more than this can he desire?

I know no better medicine against suffering injustice than to bear it in silence.

Composure and a cheerful heart are better than eating a good dinner.

To reach a worthy goal is better than to propound much wisdom.

A man must stand on his own feet before he soars aloft. If he feed his fancy and let his reason hunger he will float in thin air.

If your eyes are always fixed on the far horizon, you are likely to tumble down the stairs underfoot.

Head and heart must ever be in the right spot, but never in too many spots at once. It is best to keep one's wits about one.

To exhaust the limits of goodness, one must risk appearing wicked.

If you learn to walk by stumbling, you will do well; but if you learn to stumble by falling, things will go ill with you.

It is a good thing to repent of error; but I cannot and will not ever rue a deed undertaken in reason and justice. If any of its consequences bring me pain, this is truly cause for sorrow; but I shall never regret having acted reasonably and fairly.

The man who amasses goods and chattels with no intention of self-improvement is like a dog that gathers bones he does not eat.

Arrogance never plagues you so much as when you are stuck in the mire. So long as things go well and no one doubts that you are on top, you are unlikely to put on airs; but when the gloating scoffer spreads the news on every hand that things are not what they used to be with you, then your blood stirs and boils, and seethes like butter in the frying pan.

The faults and follies of our lives grow tainted because we are not honest with ourselves and remain content to nibble at what we dare not swallow whole.

A man never knows on his own when he is acting selfishly. He always imputes to himself motives nobler than those that actually move him.

There are always plenty of pretexts in this world for acting against our better knowledge or our conscience.

People are led by custom and by catchwords, but facts they are wont to overlook.

For the sake of our avowed purpose, we deck ourselves in delusions that we are then likely to retain unwittingly.

Fame gathers doubly over the grave of him who shunned it while alive.

If you would embitter your life, all you need do is to become embittered over things that do not go as you wish.

You feel sincerely sorry when your desires have over-powered your reason—that is, if you are serious about not playing the fool, the rogue, or the scoundrel. When such feelings of regret are strong and genuine enough, they amount to penitence.

To look at things resolutely, to observe them con-stantly, to survey them often, to look around you widely, and to consider carefully, will make you judge more justly than the best of catechisms.

Happy the man who can adjust his wants to what he has, who can renounce selfish personal desires with-out the sacrifice of either his comfort or his peace of mind.

To be happy, a man must not only be well provided for; he must also think he is well provided for.

If he is not to be unhappy, man must either over-come his desires, or boldly seek to satisfy them.

Unless he is at inward peace, man's path is full of turmoil. The thirst for the unattainable robs him of the enjoyment of near and present blessings, saps his power of wisdom, patience and adaptation.

The man who lightly flutters about the outskirts of knowledge, rather than fortifying his understanding by quiet, steady application, loses touch with Nature, foregoes real and constructive insight, and relinquishes that sense of truth that is alone receptive to true happiness.

An intimate relationship in its full power is always a source of human wisdom and strength in relationships less intimate.

From my earliest boyhood I was impressed with the sacrosanct character of humble service from the ground up. But now I have learned that if one would accomplish miracles, one must serve humbly, even when one's hair is gray.

III

Home and Hearth

III · HOME AND HEARTH

My COUNTRY, what you are, you are not by the grace of kings, nor by the power of your great men, nor by the wisdom of your sages, but by the lofty strength and wisdom of the homes of your people throughout the land.

Life shapes us. A background of grandeur tends to make us masterful; a homely background, kind.

A perfect sense of truth may grow in narrow circumstances; true wisdom rests on the firm ground of an understanding of our most immediate concerns, and a carefully nurtured capacity for managing our most personal affairs.

God ordains that mankind should learn the most important things at the fireside.

To content his heart, a man must have something in the way of a hearth that never grows cold; and that he finds in his home. Here he can relax and warm himself. Thus refreshed he can return to the woods and fields, to whatever task may be his calling. It is at home that he will be drawn to whatever there is for him to do of good and right in the most distant corner of the world. The brotherhood of man cannot grow in the untended soil of a rootless life; it must be watched and cared for at home, as the delicate garden plant needs watching and care in the greenhouse. But once it has safely sprouted there, you may transplant it to any soil you wish, and it will flourish.

Unless truth, strength, and happiness dwell in the homes of the people, they will be lacking in the life of the people as well, and the people will not be truly civilized.

Scatter or befoul the nest of a bird—and you will have undone the bird's life; but leave the people their homes in the midst of havoc—and the people will live.

The ancients held the domestic hearth sacred. A woman at her hearth, they held, who thought first of her husband and her children—the home of such a woman would surely be hallowed and blessed. Think how a wife can sway a husband who sees, from the soup she cooks and the stocking she knits for him, that, as she cooks and knits, he is ever present in her mind!

To inherit a well-ordered household is as good as to inherit goods and chattels.

Verily, verily, like unto the cradle in which the poor little Savior was laid, seem to me the homes of the people. They are the cradle in which mankind's sacred and divine heritage may sprout and grow to fullness.

In a man's growth, domestic lore is what the trunk is to a tree, for on it, all the twigs and branches of our human wisdom and destiny must be grafted. When the trunk is weak and rotten, the grafts and scions will wither.

That perfect love of God and of our neighbor, which is so essential a requirement of our nature, grows most perfectly in the devout and gladsome enjoyment of our family life.

Man's domestic joys are the best that earth affords, and the joy of parents in their children is the most hallowed joy of all. It renders parents' hearts devout and good, and raises up the children to their Father in Heaven.

A sense of fatherhood makes rulers, and one of brotherhood makes citizens; both of them work for order, in the home, and in the nation.

The man who seeks to rule as a father before he has learned to love as a brother will never be a patriarch.

Justice, as between parents and their children, can never be carried to as fine a point as can the law between horse-traders and grain-merchants.

For children, the teachings of their parents will always be the core, and as for the schoolmaster, we can give thanks to God if he is able to put a decent shell about the core.

As a mother is the first to nourish her child's body, so should she, by God's order, be the first to nourish his mind.

The lesson of the heart is brief. If only the strings of a mother's heart are touched, howsoever, her heart will come to independent life, and will beat whither it must, impelled by God.

Love has never been inspired save by love, nor has faith been won excepting by faith; it is the music in the mother's soul that calls forth the response in her child's heart.

But it is not enough that she encourage and foster her child's love and faith, she must also exalt them.

Know ye not that the bodies of your children are a temple of the Holy Spirit?

Live for your children! Become divine through them!

The love they feel for their parents has saved countless children from evil in the hour of temptation.

Praise no man for his wisdom and his virtue until you have seen how he cares for his children, and how they have repaid their father's care.

26

"A man may become a thousand things, and a child must be prepared for anything," so say we young folk, as we dream up pictures of a humanity we do not know. But in the meantime we do not trouble about the youngster we call Hans, and the boy grows up worthless because we, befogged by our humanitarian dreams, forget the real Hans, whom we set out to educate, and who has in the meantime grown to manhood.

If a man care not to be good and true for his own sake, he ought to care for his children's sake.

The most sensible parents, and the ones who do best in bringing up their children, are those who make the least use of those well-worn pedagogical phrases: "Be good, be obedient, be industrious." They stimulate the child's obedience without talking much about it; they touch his heart without telling him "be merciful"; they get him to work without saying "work brings bread"; they make him love his parents without having to say "you should" or "you must."

O blooming youth, our hope and pride! You are like a garden in all its glory. But mind you that the world is fed by the fruits of the field, not by the flowers of the garden. Get ready, then, for the day when, without adornment, you must attend to the real business of your life!

IV

The Education
of Man

IV · THE EDUCATION OF MAN

THE HIGHER PURPOSE of education is to prepare the individual to make free and self-reliant use of all the faculties with which the Creator has endowed him, and so to direct these faculties that they may perfect all human life; each individual, in his proper place, should be able to act as the instrument of the omnipotent, all-knowing Power that has called him into being.

The essence of training man's nature is to educate mankind to understanding love.

What else is education but the reverent joining of the past to the gloom of the future by making wise use of the present?

Nature endows even the best heads and hearts with no more than a disposition to teach; it is for us to develop and vitalize this uncommon disposition needed in education, as we would in the case of any other profession.

A beast is perfectly adapted to anything it may have to do; but a man is not fit for anything save what he can learn, and love, and practice.

Education is an unbroken chain of measures that all spring from the same principle, namely, an understanding of the immutable laws that govern our nature. These measures are undertaken in a uniform spirit of good-will and firmness, and they all lead to the same end, which is to exalt mankind to a dignity in keeping with his nature.

Education is nothing more than the polishing of each single link in the great chain that binds humanity together and gives it unity. The failings of education and human conduct spring as a rule from our disengaging a single link and giving it special treatment as though it were a unit in itself, rather than a part of the chain. It is as though we thought the strength and utility of the link came from its being silver-plated, gilded, or even jeweled, rather than from its being joined unweakened to the links next to it, strong and supple enough to share with them the daily stresses and strains of the chain.

The material with which the educator works, which he must be able to mold in true creative fashion, is man himself, the masterpiece of Creation. It is man whom the educator must understand—man in his full scope and power—as a gardener wisely tends the rarest plants, from their first sprouting to the maturing of their fruit. The teacher must be capable of watching man's development, whatever direction it may take, whatever the circumstances. No profession on earth calls for a deeper understanding of human nature, nor for greater skill in guiding it properly.

Pity the educator who feels he needs only to practice patience. What he really needs is a sense of love and happiness.

Teaching, by itself and in itself, does not make for love, any more than it makes for hatred. That is why teaching is by no means the essence of education. It is love that is its essence. Love alone is the eternal effluvium of the divinity that is enthroned within us. It is the central point from which the essentials of education flow.

Without love, neither the physical nor the intellectual powers of the child will develop naturally. That is only human.

Learning is not worth a penny when courage and joy are lost along the way.

The heart alone can guide the heart.

The crowning achievement of education is to reach the child's heart to convince him of our fervent love at the very moment when we are pointing out mistakes and are seeking to break a bad habit. In their mistakes, the people are very much like children too.

33

The unspoiled innocence of Nature is receptive to any impression of truth and virtue. It is like a soft wax tablet.

Nature has enclosed man's higher aptitudes as in a shell; if you break the shell before it opens on its own, you will find only a budding pearl. You will have destroyed the treasure you should have preserved for your child.

A beam must be designed for strength, and a board must not be planed too thin to suit the purpose for which it is intended. Nor must people be polished to the point of losing their sturdiness.

You must bend your children in the direction they must go almost before they know the difference between right and left. They will thank you to the end of their days that they have been trained for good ends and fitted to the yoke of our wretched life, before they knew why it was being done.

God knows, in childhood it is the little things that count. Whether a child get up half an hour earlier or later; whether it fling its Sunday clothes into a corner the whole week through, or neatly fold them up; whether it fairly dole out its bread and meal and butter for the coming week, or heedlessly devour them; it is little things like this that can bring a wife with a heart of gold to the greatest misery, and her husband and children with her.

34

In the world as it is, a man will learn only through necessity, or through conviction.

A man will never properly learn his trade in jest and fun.

The foundation for a good school is like that for any kind of happiness; it is nothing else but true wisdom in living.

If a child is to learn more than his father can teach him, his teacher must fit his supplementary instruction into what the father does at home, much as a weaver works an ornamental flower into the pattern of his cloth.

In my opinion, school instruction that fails to include the full spirit education demands, and that ignores the circumstances in the home in their entirety, is little more than a method for shriveling up our generation.

The instruction of the young must in every aspect be directed more toward developing their abilities than toward the enrichment of their knowledge.

Ignorance is better than knowledge that is but prejudice, a glass through which to view the world. To arrive at knowledge slowly, by one's own experience, is better than to learn by rote, in a hurry, facts that other people know, and then, glutted with words, to lose one's own free, observant and inquisitive ability to study.

Perhaps the most fateful gift an evil genius could bestow upon our times is knowledge without skill.

The man who has much knowledge must be guided more intently and artfully than his less learned fellow toward understanding himself, toward harmonizing his knowledge with his circumstances, and toward developing all his intellectual powers uniformly. If this is not done, his knowledge will be but a will-o'-the-wisp that will disrupt his inner life and deprive him of the essential satisfactions which a simple, straightforward purpose in harmony with itself vouchsafes the most common man.

We carry too heavy a burden of what we have neglected by way of better and more needful things.

Not art, not books, but life itself is the true basis of teaching and education.

What use is all his knowledge to a man who does not know whence his daily bread is to come?

The contrast between knowing and doing is like that between heaven and earth. Whoever confines his trade to knowledge must indeed take care that he forget not the habit of action.

Knowing and doing condition each other like a river and a spring. Without knowledge there can be no action. But as the hidden spring comes to light in the

36

river, diffusing its blessings wherever its waters flow, so must a man's knowledge come to the surface in his actions, spreading its beneficence wherever it takes effect.

Merely to know is little enough for a man; becoming used to knowledge is everything.

Life shapes us, and the life that shapes us is not a matter of words but of action—it is reality.

A man learns by action and is cheered by action—have done with words!

O holy action, mother of deeds! It is inaction that begets misdeeds.

The tenderest hand grows tough at the anvil, the lathe, the reaper, and the press. The harder you work at your chosen calling, the sooner will your hand grow hard, so that labor does not torment you.

All that a man does bears fruit; inaction alone is barren. This is the motto of noble minds and nowhere does it apply so strikingly as in the case of children.

Our powers of understanding are best developed in business affairs, where every blunder and every omission shows up on the spot, for which men should thank God. In matters of opinion and literature, on the other hand, we can go on for all eternity, twisting and turning the words in our mouths.

A hundred men will sharpen their swords, a thousand will hone their knives, yet ten thousand will fail to whet their wits, leaving them to rust in idleness.

Real truth, and genuine cheerfulness, are made up of perfection—perfection means completion. Whoever carries anything, let it be ever so little, to perfection, is secure for life.

V

Man among Men

V · MAN AMONG MEN

As long as we live, we are part of the people. We do wrong to keep ourselves aloof, and by that very act make ourselves a useless burden to the world.

One of the first lessons of my life was that a man will best advance in the path of righteous truth, if, day after day, he comes to see his limitations; if, day after day, he becomes aware of what others know better than he—in what ways their experience, skill, and mastery exceed his own.

When you know how to help yourself, few others will have power over you; but if you be of a helpless nature, you will readily come under the influence of someone who offers you a hand and undertakes to guide you, and then will really take you where he wants to go.

In the building of the world, the only stone that is of value is one that has been ground to fit.

Woe to the fool who entertains the hope that the world may yet acknowledge the real worth of any man whom it has once ground into the dust.

41

Grieve you may—you who are misunderstood—but do not let your grief embitter you! Grief that exalts and ennobles is sacred; but grief that embitters you is like a poison that eats away all virtue within you.

A mountain that rolls its rocks down on your roof is less dangerous than a neighbor who likes to gossip to the judge.

If we could but have a glimpse inside the homes of our enemies, about whom we rant with such wrath and passion; if we could but witness their troubles and sufferings, we should grow ashamed at the many things we have been innocently ready to believe of them.

If we would only find it in ourselves to spread the news of the good qualities of our neighbors, of their repentance, as swiftly and with the same satisfaction as when we gossip about their failings! Do we not owe this to our neighbor who has turned over a new leaf?

What nonsense to try to measure international preponderance or equilibrium! We must throw the weight of all of us into the balance, otherwise we shall weigh nothing in the scales of Europe.

If apology neither reconciles the injured party, nor bespeaks repentance in the detractor, then it is not only vain, but assuredly harmful.

Genuflection I do not hold to be harmful for those

who bend the knee, but most pernicious for those who keep their feet, and for the republican spirit generally.

A good word will always find a good place in which to say it.

 The best way to get people to speak up is to set their minds at rest.

When people inflict great wrongs upon one another, you are likely to hear it said afterward, "If only they had talked it over first!"

What comes from the heart will reach the heart.

Quiet sympathy touches the heart more than many words.

The greatest blessing on the death-bed is a reconciliation; the prayers of a dying man for his unforgiving foe are, like the glory of the sunrise, a foretaste of the heavenly life to come.

The art of inflicting punishment consists often enough in pleading the right excuses; the art of protecting oneself against thieves and rascals, in understanding and granting what rightfully belongs to all; the art of piling on a load, in a proper knowledge of the beast that must bear the burden.

It is not necessity that brutalizes people, it is highhandedness, passion, the meanness with which people embitter their lives, that brutalizes our inner feelings.

The man who forever complains gives little thought to how he could do better; he always looks to others, or even to the Government. Does such a man really love his country?

To believe that order and obedience make for peace and happiness—that is education for social life.

The alpha and omega of my politics is education.

States may bloom and perish as does a man; they are, indeed, nothing other than a man, blooming and perishing in the open, employing his powers in unity with others for his good, or for his ruin.

Mankind in the mass has no virtues; only the individual has them. The state as such has none; it merely has the power to use the virtues of its individual members.

Governments are always much more likely to go astray than men. Instinct never impels a society, and where it is ineffective, truth will only come into half its rights.

My country! My country! The value to the state of your citizens is no whit greater than their value to themselves. Any faith in the civic value of a citizen who sets no individual value on himself is a dream from which you will some day awake in terror. Any country, but especially a free country, is socially in good health only because of the moral, spiritual and civic virtues of the individuals that make it up.

Just as no royal government can be good without respect for the throne and the king's will, so can no republican government be good without respect for the middle classes and the people's will.

He who does not love his people is unworthy of them. He who looks down on his people will not rule them well. Though he give away his property and go to the stake himself for them, he will not rule them well.

According to all the precepts, it is quite easy to train men in great bodies for almost any purpose you will—to hunt wild beasts, and even to track down beggars and other human beings. But to see that these trained creatures remain human, and righteous, and good—that is, in truth, not easy, nor can it be expected to be so.

Resort to violence is no means of government; neither is an axe, whose use is to cut down trees, a means to plant a forest.

A man cannot be Pope without his favorites, nor King without his slaves; the lowest of their agents will be King or Pope to the people, unless the people count for more than they.

If you wish thoroughly to debauch a man and ruin him completely—unless he is good through and through —you have only to give him an office in which he can spy out the weaknesses and follies of his fellow men.

It is a well-known fact that of all tyrants the smallest are the cruelest; but of all petty tyrants, school tyrants are the worst.

The first attribute of government is to safeguard the hearts of one's fellow men. The man who cannot do this will rule with the scepter in his left hand.

A man who is merely a good man should never seek to govern, and never, never, should he seek to place himself above another.

It takes much wisdom, but little wine, to make people satisfied.

The peoples of Europe receive public training in no skills save that of mass-murder, the military organization of which swallows up everything that is owed the people—or rather, that the people owe themselves.

The sword will nevermore help mankind to attain its true rights. Down the ages human rights in their sacred perfection issue only from truth in love.

Revolutions are like a water wheel, for in the end they always bring the worst mistakes of human nature to the top.

If a pond grow foul, what if a few dozen fish in it still remain healthy?

Everything must some day be renewed. But a man who is restoring something must take care that he does not pour out the child with the bath water. On a sound wall, the stucco will often weather a hundred times before the wall itself decays. The man would be a fool who tore down a wall because the stucco on it had crumbled away, and so would he who cut down a healthy tree because of its mossy bark. To replace a tree may take a generation, and to restore a state, I think, will take a like time. We must always remember that not everyone who can repair an old wall can build a new one; and people who pour out the child with the bath water are worthless for purposes of regeneration.

Let us hold sacred the oath we have sworn to God and to our country, rather to suffer wrong than to do wrong, and always to couple love of truth and justice with love of peace and harmony.

I believe it to be the essence of true morality to suffer wrong rather than to do wrong.

VI

Of Poverty,
the Sacred

VI · OF POVERTY, THE SACRED

TROUBLE TEACHES US TO PRAY; it sharpens our senses, stimulates our limbs, and what is most important, it touches our hearts and stirs the noblest sentiments in our nature.

The eye of the sufferer is the widest open for truth.

Trouble is no respecter of our failings. If you are in difficulties, you may try to fool yourself by finding a thousand excuses for your mistakes, but you will soon see that this does no good at all. You must use your head and hands, and take hold where the shoe pinches.

You will always find that the man who has experienced sorrow and trouble is apt to be more of a man than the fellow who has had none—that he can do more, and that he will be more.

Trouble and poverty bring many things into your head and hands that you must work over with patience and hard effort until they yield you bread.

Life's troubles cut deeply into the purity of the human heart. If you give a poor man bread, you will diminish, in yourself as well as him, the inclination to grow obdurate and inwardly brutal that comes from his troubles.

The man who cannot share the poor man's bread, on him God has conferred a boon, but it is a boon given in wrath.

A man cannot become a man when he is sunk in the morass of misery.

The spectacle of trouble fires our hearts, but unless the emergency is extreme, we are likely to bargain with ourselves and with our humanity until we cool off and then generally do nothing.

Does the glimmer of pity we feel for capital misfortune and spectacular suffering really blunt our feeling for daily misery and want?

Even in the deepest depravity of our nature, the light of God, which is everlasting, is never extinguished in the human soul.

The sufferings of a man who truly loves his God and his neighbor will not succeed in making him miserable; rather will they strengthen him, build up his inner powers, and exalt him even above his troubles.

Rich and poor alike must have the heart in the right spot if they are to be happy; and far more people attain this end through care and want than through peace and joy. Otherwise God would surely have been glad to provide us nothing but pleasure. But since people can endure good fortune, peace, and happiness only when their hearts are inured to self-control, when they are steadfast, strong, patient, and wise, it follows of necessity that there must be much misery and suffering in the world.

God has turned the Devil loose lest we become devils.

The seeds of truth and justice sprout in the hallowed hovels of the poor, where want and misery cultivate the soil so thoroughly, far more freely than in the halls of men who know constraint and force, not from having suffered them, but only from having exercised them.

Need and deathbed assemble a hundred hearts where joy and pleasure gather only one.

He who finds not wisdom at the deathbed of a dear one, finds it nowhere on earth.

God's school, necessity, will make a mother doubly a mother, and a child twice over a child.

Through love, you shall bear sufferings like a treasure from the Lord; your strength and your benison shall grow under the load you carry.

My heart is gripped to see how humanity matures to immortality in the dust, and how amid luxury and trifles it will wither unrewarded.

THE EDUCATION OF MAN

The world grows poor in seeking to avoid poverty; the man who strives for riches most earnestly is seen to be the poorest.

The man who enjoys his pittance in peace and happiness is most evidently rich.

The only true charity is so contrived that the recipient need beg no more.

Whoever is unwilling to help himself can be helped by no one.

We must help a poor man not to lose heart, to try with all his might to get back on his feet; the gift that makes him negligent and lazy, that lets him rot in his own filth, as it were, not only is no charity, but actually debars him from regaining his strength.

It is important that my people keep up their spirits, and therefore it surely is not sinful even for a poor man to put a chicken in the pot on occasion, to give pleasure to his wife.

An unspoiled man is cheerful and grateful. He knows no greater pleasure than to provide a happy hour for those who have to bear life's burdens with him.

The true public charity which the officials and teachers ought to provide for the good folk in their humble cottages, is this; themselves to light the sacrificial fire of love in every village, that the common

people in the land may once more lend one another
more assistance, help, and comfort. If we had that, I
should gladly remit to the officials all unspent relief
funds.

Strive from your childhood to honor God in the
poor, and for the sake of God to see the lowliest of
men as your brethren, your friends, your neighbors.

As a man improves and hallows himself, so will he
make himself helpful. Hallowed and helpful—the two
words almost mean the same.

One profound experience I have made: the human
heart—even the heart of Government, the hardest of
them all—cannot bear to see any great and honest
sacrificial effort go helplessly to waste, come to an
untimely end, when once its buds have been seen to
come to open bloom.

Misfortune must be tackled with hands and feet,
not with the mouth.

A coat of paint will not make old walls new, nor a
rotten rope strong again.

You can describe the night, and paint the black-
ness of its shadows, but this will help no one to see it;
only when you light a candle can you show what the
night was like, and only when you lance a cataract can
you show what blindness meant.

55

Anyone but a fool will, when he sees the people suffering, go after the mice that nest in the darkness under the floor, where they nibble at the tender roots of the people's well-being, and end by ruining them.

If you would drain a swamp, do not wallow in the mire, but lower the level of water and provide good drainage.

"You can't change human nature!"—As long as the world has stood, stupid people, and sly, have worked hand in glove and used these words to unstring the bow, whenever some constructive project did not happen to suit their purpose.

Let no one tell me any longer that you cannot help the people—you do not *want* to help them. The means to do so lie at the heart of the people's misery. It is the simplest thing on earth—but you learn it by doing it.

VII

Justice and
Liberty

VII · JUSTICE AND LIBERTY

THOU GUARDIAN SPIRIT OF THE LAND! Thunder aloud the everlasting verity, that liberty for all means guarding the rights of all!

Charters and seals, rights and privileges, must prove their value in the cottage of the common man, in his barns and chests, on his table, and in his chamber.

Justice, if it lack a sense of brotherhood, is a glittering monstrosity, without power to do good.

Man is a sublime miracle in the somber chaos of mysterious Nature. He alternates forever between killing off his happiness by appealing to his rights, and undermining his rights by claiming happiness. And so he wanders on, wretched and disfranchised, bearing within himself the blame for his exhaustion.

Justice is something a man must seek, but happiness comes to him who waits.

The sense of suffering injustice does more harm in the world than any other thing. There is one common experience in my life of which I am sure. The hearts of those who have been unjustly accused are so sickened that, in their own failings, they will forever cling to the false charges that have been made against them, the injustice they have suffered, more and more obscuring their true shortcomings.

It is in the deepest abyss of injustice that you will always find the most painstaking care to prevent a semblance of justice.

He who has filled his pockets in the service of injustice will have little good to say on behalf of justice.

Only when the poor and wretched readily have their day in court, can justice be said to prevail in the land.

It is a shame that we always let the weeds shoot up until they have taken hold; then, with officious righteousness, we root among the outraged people like a pig in the cornfield, and make out that with such tomfoolery we have attained the heights of civic achievement.

A dog might say: He who cringes in the presence of the great, and yelps against the little ones, will surely achieve his ends.

The individual authority of high-minded, wise, and godly men of all degrees, holds a powerful force against the iniquities of our rulers and officials—a force that is founded on human justice and blessed by God.

There can be no law among nations without law within nations, nor can there be justice for the people without respect for the rights of man.

If you show him love, and guide him toward faith in our Heavenly Father, a man will be more likely to keep away from evil, than if you fill the land with jails and gallows.

Our hearts are inexorably touched when we consider that punishment and retribution never make men better unless they are accompanied by kindness and by love.

Truly, we must begin with the breadbasket if we would make decent laws, especially if we would put an end to the transgressions of the people, and the extortions that suck dry the land. Where there is despondency and hunger, half the people are quite likely to end up in infamy, without effort.

Exemption from due punishment where punishment is merited, unsullied honor where disgrace is called for, are like poison in a dish of sweets; you eat of it to your heart's content, and then go on to irreparable perdition.

Save two pennies from childhood; this is a remedy against the causes of crime that otherwise call for the gallows and the rack.

Man is disfranchised and made distraught because

he does not care for truth and justice. But he will find truth if he seek it. He will have justice, if he desire it.

One of the baneful misjudgments of my time is that it has been thought so easy to cover up injustice with good deeds.

Why must there be streams of blood, when a people wishes to be free? The reason is clear enough; the strong think it is their right to subjugate the weak until the weak in turn become strong. This generally comes about because the strong drive the weak to fury by unreasonable demands, making them aware of a power they did not know they possessed.

Least of all is liberty the right to do what is not prohibited by law. It is, on the contrary, the citizen's lawful power to do what will enhance his happiness, and to restrain what is likely to do him harm.

Do not deceive yourself, my country! Our children will not find liberty dropping like a plum into their open mouths, any more than it has thus come to any other country. There may be children of fortune who find riches flying in by the window, but peoples and nations are seldom happier than they deserve to be.

Liberty is mere talk where people have lost their sensibilities, where their understanding has not been fed by knowledge, and their power of judgment has been neglected—most of all, however, where they are unmindful of their rights and duties as moral beings.

Truth is not a one-sided thing. Liberty is a boon, and obedience likewise. We must join what Rousseau sundered.

True liberty makes us modest and high-minded, rather than brazen.

Some folk, in their zeal for liberty, want to set a fire in the rooftree, but others prefer it in the stove.

Am I mistaken when I think that people who yearn for liberty are easy to lead to civic virtue?

Men care not for liberty if they be contented; and even if the measure of their happiness be but half full, they love their peace and their pantry too much to gamble with them.

A land is badly off in every way if it respect its rights and privileges only because they tickle its pride.

Misguided nations cling desperately to such words as "Country," "King," and "Vested Right," risking life and limb, goods and chattels in their defense, even when the country is not truly theirs, even when they enjoy neither liberty, nor security, nor justice, even when self-seeking scoundrels and petty tyrants use those words against them—against freedom, truth, God, justice and the poor.

VIII

Truth and Wisdom

VIII · TRUTH AND WISDOM

TRUTH, THE DIVINE, the heavenly, shines in the firmament above us like a sacred star; a temporal truth is like a rush-light, burning only in the dark—and only because it *is* dark.

Weak eyes too may gaze at the sun, but they behold nothing but the spot it scorches on the retina. The eagle, on the other hand, sees in the sun's rays the shining path on which he may soar in its ocean of light.

The world is closer to the truth in every way than it thinks; a glimmer of the truth always hovers clear and bright before the eyes of men. It is the eyes that are at fault, for they have been spoiled for the light of truth, as the eyes of moles, from living under the earth, have been spoiled for the light of the sun.

It is Man's fate that no one knows the truth alone; we all possess it, but it is divided up among us. He who learns from one man only, will never learn what the others know.

The truth as understood by any one man is not the same as that of his fellow men; each man, before God, must keep his own truth, and make his peace with that which runs counter to the human element in his particular brand of truth.

He who loves truth only insofar as it is revealed in all its splendor in the less important hours of his existence, is unworthy of the truth.

Even if today we cannot gain acceptance for some salutary verity, we must not, on that account, cease to try to do so. We must strive all the harder to open the door for it tomorrow.

Who has no heart for truth, sooner or later the Devil will have his head.

When one man's thought becomes that of a hundred men, there will be a hundred thoughts instead of one, no one of which will be that of the first man whence they all issued.

Opposition brings out much more of truth and of the exercise of power than does the paltry arrogance of trying to prevail without opposition. The man who listens only to himself and to his yes-men is not worthy of those who oppose him with the truth; they can by their opposition raise him higher by as much as, without their truth, he now stands lower.

No scoundrel is so wicked that he cannot at some point truthfully reprove some honest man; there is no fool who could not on occasion give the smartest of us some good lesson.

Truth is a medicine that takes hold.

Truly, a man who has been brought to the point of seeking for the truth must be watched over like a woman in childbed. Depending on the way we treat him, the child he brings forth may be alive or stillborn.

Good humor is the seasoning of Truth.

Experience is the seal of Truth.

More often than not the truth calls attention to itself through some trifle rather than through its own merits.

This is man's way: So long as he thinks that something he does not like is not true, he will scoff at it; but when he comes to think that it might be true after all, he begins to think up reasons why it cannot be true.

People really like to believe a foolishness, and they also like to play the fool. Yet they would have their foolish beliefs and actions thought so sensible that neither angel nor devil could deny them. That is why they must so often go in wretched quest of reasons.

If you seek the truth, then do not chase after it, do not hunt for it, but wait for it, in patience, love and tranquillity. If you do that, it will come to you on its own.

A thousand times over, we seek not so much to hunt down the truth, as to get it away from someone else.

All things change save truth, and innocence, and right; these remain the same whether men respect them or not.

Truth rests on a rock as its sole foundation. A lie, however, always takes its position behind a lot of reasons, in which it hides as it were behind a heap of pebbles.

The light of truth and the flame of love light up the darkness in its furthest corners, revealing their works to the light of day.

Modesty is the mate of wisdom, and the daughter of innocence.

All human knowledge rests on the power of a good heart that seeks the truth.

IX
Chips and Shavings

IX · CHIPS AND SHAVINGS

THE GREATEST and loftiest thoughts are often robbed of their value because youthful ardor needlessly shows them off on the wrong occasion.

Premature judgments are prejudices from which error rises up as fog does from the sea.

An instrument that is out of tune insults the ear, but a discordant heart insults the soul.

A violin string that has long rusted in a corner will snap when you attempt to tighten it.

Man's virtue can be perfected, even though it be but grafted on a parent stock of greed. Even there it will bear fruit as fine as any it has ever borne.

When a man is permitted to do as he pleases, evil will flourish within him like the Cedars of Lebanon and the palms by the Brook Kidron, and the Devil will rejoice, as though the angels were napping.

No one can choose wisely excepting his knowledge range far; and no one can know much, excepting he ponder deeply; hence most people, given free choice in all things, will generally choose ill.

A wobbly table is all but useless; but a faltering man is even less useful by far, for he is harder to support.

Unless man be fully deserving of his name, all that is human crumbles in his hands; unless he muster his strength, all power is but a rope of sand; unless he be pure in heart, all love turns to wormwood.

The black man paints the Devil white, but the white man sees him black.

One man will base his conceit on his good health, another on his moneybags, and still another on the brains he fails to use.

Everywhere you go you will find it the custom for the deepest-dyed rascals to talk the loudest about their honor and their good repute.

It is generally the hypocrites and liars who complain the loudest: "O Lord, can we no longer trust any man's word?"

Even when there is honor among thieves, a hypocrite is worse than useless.

As long as they can, rascals will always pretend to have no worries.

Nothing so much disconcerts the arrogant tyrant as

when those hitherto under his thumb begin to assert their own rights.

He who degrades his fellow man to be a beggar and a knave will always be the first to call him so.

Rich rogues are always hard on poor rogues; and mighty sinners will be spiteful toward a petty culprit who is powerless.

Friendliness as a snare is far more dangerous than fear or anger. A frightened man knows he is caught; but the man who has been dazzled by a show of friendliness is blissfully unaware and never thinks of flight.

When the squire truckles to the village beggar, then God help the farmer!

Calumny is the stock-in-trade of the rabble-rouser. It mixes poison with glittering truth.

When people talk too loud or too low, it is best to give them a wide berth.

Envy makes a man crooked; he can see nothing straight, and sees himself as crooked as he does other folk.

The more deeply a man ponder, the more frugal will he be with words.

You are wroth because you cannot always say what you wish. But do not rage because at times you are forced to be wise against your will.

Many words make an excuse anything but convincing.

Words, like smoke, are a sign of fire, but not the fire itself; the cleaner the fire, the less smoke.

Who says too much, says nothing.

A sheathed sword is better than swallowed affronts; but setting out trees is better than either.

A barbed tongue is worse than a flashing sword. However deep the wound, the injured person cannot see it, and will neglect to have it cured.

Innuendo dies of inanition, unless it is fed.

Jests should never hurt, else they become insults; you can lose in jest what you might be loath to miss.

The tongue is closer to man's heart than is his hand. Art may boldly reveal the lowest depths of vice with hand and brush, but it will not profane the heart with the same power as does the tongue when, with similar boldness, it shows us vice unveiled.

The man too keenly aware of his good reputation is likely to have a bad one.

To a woman, a good name is like the halo that shines about a saint.

A man who has his failings is lucky if jealousy assails him at a point where he is innocent, and all the more so if it seizes on matters of little moment.

When books are treated right, a woman should then find them to be like her Sunday clothes, while her chores are like her working dress.

The goodness of a man is like the sun at noon, but that of a woman is like the dawn and the evening twilight.

Gratitude is not a weed that will grow in any soil; it is a tender plant, that will no more grow in hard and arid soil than it will in swampy ground.

When the milk boils and threatens to run over, then the women merely pour in a few drops of cold water.

When one goose cackles, they all will cackle.

An ass remains an ass, do with him and bridle him as you will.

Great men never tell you how great they are; but it is inherent in the pettiness of little folk that they desire to be great.

As the light grows dimmer if the candles are not trimmed, so will the world's great luminaries darken too, if no one take issue with them.

Fashions are usually seen in their true perspective only when they have gone out of fashion.

A feeling for order, harmony, beauty and peace is the sensible basis of morality.

Cleanliness, order, and care will safeguard virtue as the armor protects a man of war.

A penny saved by industry and order is worth more than a dollar gained by knavery and unruliness.

Thrift saves us from borrowing; but borrowing will often rob us of the means to save.

A mended woolen smock is better than a silken robe that has not been paid for.

Ownership is a fine thing. Man alone owns things— and man alone owes debts.

Sharing shows what people are, but it is possession that makes them what they are.

It is a nasty business, to dig out one's food with one's nails—but it is nastier still to dig out maliciously from the beautiful and good those infirmities that may still be in it.

The man who has achieved great clarity can afford deep shadows.

A falling oak will smash itself a thousand times worse than will a toppling shrub.

As long as a man has two feet that are unlike, he must also have two different shoes.

Not everything that towers over something else is for that reason better than the thing it overtops.

The man who lets you chop wood on his back is likely to get it in the neck.

Soft wood is easy to work.

A thing that nobody looks for is seldom found.

There are cases when healthy common sense and a warm heart will get you further than a highly cultivated, cool, and calculating mind.

The hand and the heart will both of them play tricks with you, unless you are always at their heels.

Nature will not have man live by bread alone, nor will she have him live by his heart alone; he must live by all that is in him, and about him—by every word that has come to him from the lips of God. That this belief is true is shown us by our own nature which we cannot gainsay, for it will bring weariness of mind to all who do not live according to this order.

Much in this world comes hard to us only so long as we do not sensibly and seriously try to master it.

The powers of our nature are lost to us a thousand times more often because we let them stand and go to rust unused, than because we break them by overtaxing them, or wear them out by long continuous use.

Nobody does more to spoil our general intentions than the dreamy-eyed dealers in generalities, and no one will advance them more than a wide-awake practical man.

The good stays good forever, but the bad gets worse with age.

All things bad carry their own coffins on their backs.

Nothing made of gold is consumed by fire; the blazing flame will only purify it.

A man must have some vexation; if no one else will vex him, he will vex himself.

To see a man in chains is a dreadful thing; but for every one struck in chains, a hundred lay them on themselves.

Laughter is healthy, and joy a balm; but peace of mind is the source of laughter, and the ointment-jar of joy.

Love does not rule, but it does create, and that is more.

Of a thousand spring flowers, scarcely one will ripen to autumnal fruit; of a thousand of love's embraces, scarcely one will mature into a warm and satisfying friendship.

Only in the greatest souls does love develop into

saving friendship; without self-knowledge and strength, without wisdom, patience, and inward dignity, love remains but the feeble bond of happy days gone by. It will dissolve as soon as the unsavory waters of affliction pour on it, and the storms of life, testing the mettle of a man, come rushing on.

We Swiss are lost if we lose that heritage from our fathers, their homesickness.

X

*Nature,
the World,
and God*

X · NATURE, THE WORLD, AND GOD

THE SUN has one kind of brightness, the moon another, the stars each in their own degree: but it takes all of them together to make up the fair sky.

What a world is this! Next to the kennel stands a garden, and out on the meadow malodorous refuse lies side by side with rich fodder. A curious world indeed, for even the lovely meadows would yield us no fodder, were it not for the manure we spread on them.

Rejoice to be alive, my child. Think on it often—how good it is to be alive on earth. When the smiling sun rises for you in the morning, when in nightly solitude, beneath the moon and the stars, you think of your God, when you frolic in the joys of harvest-time and the pleasure of wintry games, then feel the deep warmth of being alive, of drinking in the delights of this fair earth.

God's earth is fair, on every hand Nature tenders us joy and pleasure. But man's delight is greater than all the beauties of the earth.

As a man grows in goodness, as friendship and love

refine him to gentleness, so will the beauties and blessings of Nature awaken his love and resolution.

All that happens in Nature is everlastingly interwoven. Yet, save for a few traces, the secret of Nature's threads, of her warp and woof, of her ultimate ends, is hidden from us. Consider the spider as she spins her web, and compare her art with that of man. You will find that to the spider the Creator gave her art entire, while to man he gave but the bias.

The finger of God is shrouded in mystery, and the substance of His nature is veiled in everlasting darkness. To the eye of man, nothing of the life of Creation is visible except a tiny corner of the billowing carpet that is spread over the surface of the globe.

Nature is of God, and the eternal and divine in human nature is higher and more God-like than all the rest of Creation. The divine element in human nature is as everlasting as God himself. Though the clouds in the sky may darken, what does that matter to the eternal stars?

All man's life on earth is but a stage in his education, in which his powers and aptitudes are developed for all eternity in accordance with the Creator's will.

Man lives forever but in the divine, the God-like, that is in his nature, and only in and through this is he immortal. Whatever he may have in common with the physical side of Creation lends no value to his humanity, and least of all justifies a claim to immortality.

God is of men, for men, and by men. Man knows God only as he knows mankind, that is to say, himself. He reveres God only as he respects himself, that is to say, to the degree that he applies the best and purest instincts that are in him to himself and his fellow men. Hence, one man should lift up another to the teachings of religion, not by means of words and pictures alone, but by his acts. It is vain to tell the poor man "There is a God," and to say to the orphan "You have a Father in Heaven," for no man can teach another to know God by words and pictures alone. But if you help the poor man to live once again like a human being, then indeed do you show him God. And if you bring up the little orphan as though he had a father, you teach him to know his Father in Heaven, who so molded your heart that you could not but play father to the orphan.

Love, trust, gratitude, and the practice of obedience, must have developed within me before I can apply them to God. I must love mankind, I must trust men, I must be grateful to men, I must obey men, before I can bring myself to love God, to trust Him, thank Him, and obey Him. "For he that loveth not his brother whom he hath seen, how can he love God whom he hath not seen?"

Belief in God, thou art graven in the nature of mankind. Like the sense of good and evil, like the inextinguishable feeling for right and wrong, so dost thou lie unchangeably firm in the innermost recesses of our nature, the foundation on which we become men.

O Man, your inner feeling is the surest lodestar of truth and duty; can you still doubt, since this feeling speaks to you so loudly of immortality?

Believe in yourself, O Man—believe in the inner meaning of your being. Then will you believe in God and immortality.

The inner truth of Nature, which God with his eternal stylus has inscribed in the hearts of men, is in divine and everlasting harmony with the verities of religion and of the Gospels.

As the baby at the mother's breast, in full enjoyment of his bliss, smiles up to her his faith, so does man on earth offer up his faith to the Almighty.

The traces of the Lord's bounty, and the footprints of the Almighty in the dust, are different in each corner of the world. Thus will the image of the Eternal also differ everywhere.

Let no one quarrel with his brother about what lies

beyond the grave, which is God's business. God will reveal it all to each of us that loves him, when the hour strikes at which it will be meet for us to know it.

Let us spare the feelings of the devout, even if we ourselves do not believe.

O you men! However you may differ in serving the Lord, you will always serve him rightly if you abide as children of your Father, if you love and help one another to sanctify the dissimilar service of your God in the universal harmony of your love of man.

What can a mortal say of God, what can he tell of Him, other than "He is good, He is the Father, I thank Him and I thank Him."

What is Man, and what is his conceit, that he dare speak like an eyewitness of Heaven which he sees but through a glass darkly, arching overhead, above the earth, his dwelling-place? Let him thank God that he beholds a sun beyond the grave; let him fall to his knees in prayer, dazzled by its brightness. His fellows shall rejoice in his prayer, prostrate themselves in turn, and worship the sun that shines beyond the grave. And if a man stand beside him, and say unto him, "I see other shapes and hues and figures beyond the mist," let him take care that he rise not up from his adoration and deny the man that says this.

Those who quarrel most about religion have little of it.

That which is most sublime seems so simple that children think they can do much better.

To the people, faith in God, and the teaching of his service, are matters not of the head, but of the heart. Peace of mind in the dark night, resignation to God's will in this vale of tears, a child-like respect for the Lord and Consummator of our life—these are concerns of faith, not a problem for the mind.

The Bible demands of men not the science of religion, but its practice.

The clergy should seek to bring the people not closer to the stars, but closer to humanity.

Surely the best catechism is one the children understand without their pastor.

Religion does not call people away from their worldly duties, but rather gives them strength to attend properly to men's affairs down to the last moment.

The way to Heaven is to do our duty while on earth.

Religion of itself will make no merchant, tradesman, scholar, nor artist. But it rounds out what it does not give, it hallows what it does not create, it blesses what it does not teach.

Love is made up not of words and fancies, but of man's ability to carry the world's burdens, to lessen its miseries, and to soften its distress. The God of Love made love a part of the order of things on earth, and the man who is at odds with his role in the world, will likewise be at odds with the love of God and of his neighbors. Love that is without force and effect is no love at all.

I do not think much of people whose every second word is a quotation from the Bible.

The best homily for anyone is surely one that comes directly from his heart, although the saying of an Apostle may have been ten times finer and greater—to the Apostle!

People like to think that the proper faith is the one that tickles their fancy and brings them some return.

Good old religion is made to cover everything. Even if it is only the ferment in our blood that throws men into turmoil, that makes them no wiser—in the end God and Christianity must furnish the pretext.

Religion is God's affair, but people misuse it as they do the blessings of their country, in order to oppress the poor and break the law.

Wise men calculate the worth of virtue to the penny, but Jesus teaches men to practice virtue without guile.

The Savior never played the advocate for anyone, least of all for great folk.

Where schools and churches break down, the people will likewise break down.

Religion, established through an excess of divine love, can be revived from its deep decline, which you all deplore, only by faithfully emulating the love that founded it.

To overcome one's self, to live for others, to show a cheerful disposition and grateful heart at the very brink of the grave—these show most plainly that a man has religion.

God is always close by where people show love toward one another.

Without love, a man is without God; and without both God and love, what is man?

Faith is love; and where love dwells, God has His sanctuary in our midst.

When, after long hot days, with the ground thirsting and plants languishing for water, a thunderstorm appears, the poor farmer trembles at the sight of the rising clouds. He forgets the thirsty fields and withered plants in the burning soil, and remembers only the rolling of the thunder, the havoc of the hail, the incandescent bolt of lightning, and the overwhelming flood. But He who dwells in the heavens above does not forget the thirsty fields and the withered plants in the burning soil, and His storm drenches with blessings the fields of the poor people, who at midnight, in the lightning's glare and amid the thunders of the sky, gaze in terror at the hills whence His storm has come. And in the morning, the farmer sees the prospect of his crop redoubled. He folds his hands before the Lord of All, whose thunderstorm made him tremble but an hour ago.

No, no, it was no artful pose that bent the knee of the first man who sank into the dust before the rising sun! It was a God who sent him to the dust; and he rises up more human than if he had looked it boldly in the face.

God is the father of mankind; his children are immortal.

Surely the greatest of God's teachings is that the Lord never breaks a mended pipe nor puts out a glowing wick.

Love is the bond that ties the globe together.